DIVINE:

Modern Monlams

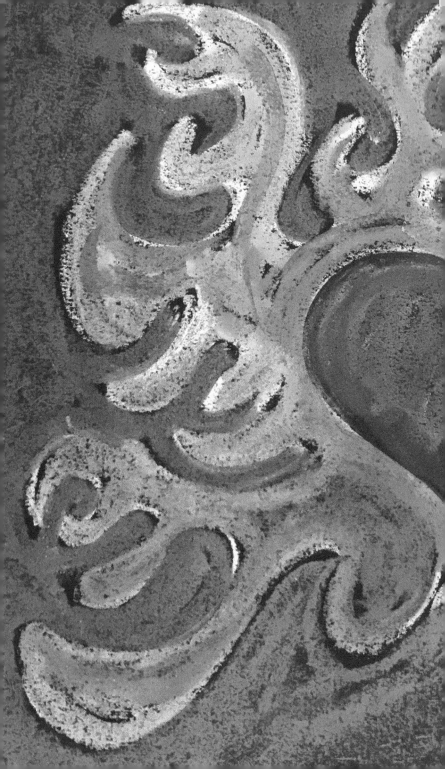

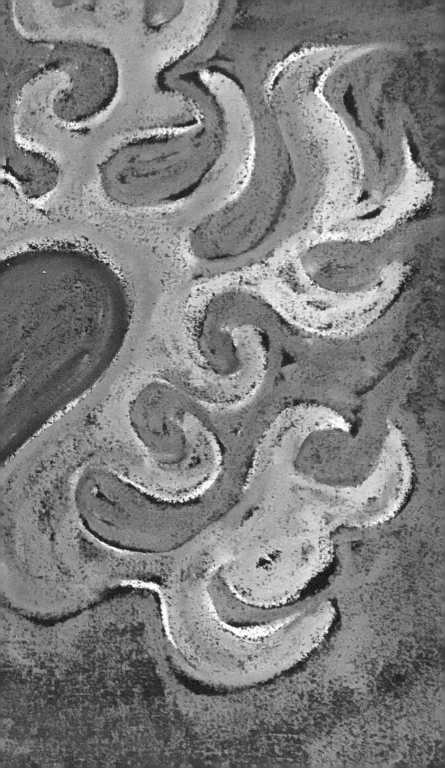

ERICSON PROPER
Creative High Growth Mentor
Transformational Coach

Typeset and designed by Ericson AF Proper
Printed in the United States

ericsonproper.com

First Published 2020

TABLE *of* CONTENTS

 Forward

The journey
begins with
a word.

A breath
of "yes".

An invitation
to meet yourself
in a sacred
space
that has been
waiting
for you to visit.

And now you are
here.
Holding these
words.

Words pulled
from the u n k   n   o   w   n

A key to
a secret world.

A recipe
for healing.

Won't you come in?

Peleg Top
Santa Fe, 2020

Illustrations and artwork by the author

Introduction

monlam — "Wish-Path"

In Tibetan, *mon* means a wish, desire, or aspiration and *lam*, a path. In the Buddhist tradition, a monlam is a skillful means practice of helping others through the intention of prayers. Each prayer is being sent to sentient beings in six realms (human, animal, hungry ghost, hell, demi-god, and god realms), which are also indicative of negative mental states.

From this perspective, this book is the compilation of the daily blessings I delivered to a group of six courageous, creative, and beautiful people, now as co-facilitator of a process that had radically altered the course of my life a mere 400 days before. It was my honor to serve anew in this pilgrimage as a guide and support in the *100 Days of Creative High Growth* created and led by Peleg Top.

In saying, "Hell, Yeah!" to assist in the process, never had it occurred to me that I would be called to dive even more deeply into the initiatory process of the 100 days than I had previously. However, the skill of every good spiritual friend, mentor, and coach is to gently nudge you into uncovering your essence and relishing your imperfect perfection even more intimately.

Peleg invited me to accept the challenge that had come to him intuitively as my part in the journey. I am no stranger to intuition — she is actively part of my soul's ecology, standing hand-in-hand with my daemon/muse. The soul's cartography is relationship-rich, and my relationship with intuition is now ever more deeply seated.

I am overjoyed to have brought this challenge to fruition. Learning to wait, rest, and listen; to tease the song from whispers and intimations; to be again broken that divine light pour through scar and wound so as to heal and give succor.

This book is the culmination and gift of this endeavor, a revelation and an individualized scripture. It is a distillation of gnosis, a personal examination, a guidebook to the psyche, a journal of pilgrimage back home to the rewilded soul, and the simple words of fool — a fool of love.

It is my aspiration that it serve as a secular book of prayer, regardless of tradition, that unites us in a common language of love, longing, and appreciation for the Mystery that is life.

Sarva Mangalam!

Ericson AF Proper
from my mountain seat, Pema Ösel Ling
Lakeland, Florida, 2020

For more information on Peleg Top and the 100 Days of Creative High Growth *process, please visit* **pelegtop.com**.

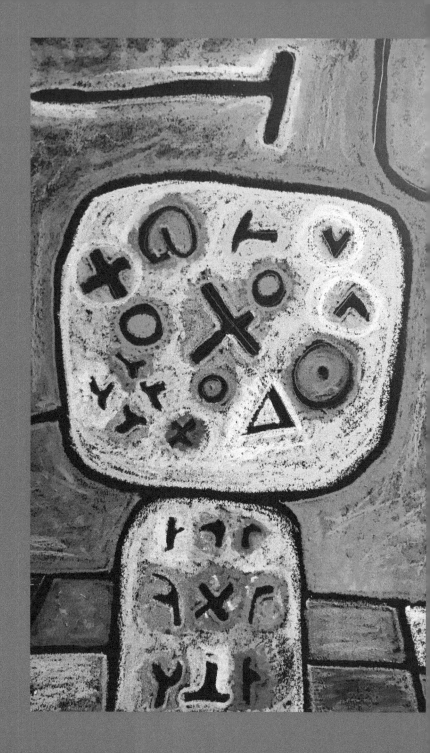

SECTION No.1

Invocation

THE URGE TO SPEAK
FROM OUR SACRED SPACES

Each of us is infused by Mystery: it is
through, with, and in us. To commence
in the essential work of self-recollection
and -love, the universal impulse arises to
ask for guidance and assistance, from those
who have achieved or tasted this state of
innate nature, wisdom, and intuiton.

Thus I invite you to slow down, relax,
and connect to your inner landscape —
the cartography of your soul.

Creative Free Spirit

Be present to this courageous one who makes
a welcome home for you today.

INSPIRE ME with spacious curiosity and wonder
as I embark into the fruitful unknown.

GUIDE ME as I openly feel into
the wide and wild spaces of self-discovery.

IMBUE ME with a most delicious trust
and fulfillment of my heart's desire.

May I experience the spontaneous joy of play
and the authentic contentment of self-love.

May I cultivate the unfathomable confidence, clarity, and insight
that comes from true self-knowledge.

May I fully reveal the radiant power and beauty of my person
and become an abundant vessel of love.

In this pilgrimage home to my deepest self:
hold me tenderly as a mother,
passionately like a lover,
and fondly as a treasured friend.

Sarva Mangalam!

May all be auspicious!

montum

I have started something new,
and trust in the magic of new beginnings.

From fear to excitement
is the practice of this journey.

The critic stands only as a guardian
until I am again ready to trust myself
and wield this power.

Underneath my doubt is the power
to create and manifest my desire.

Be my field-trip buddy on this deep dive,
and guide me to your treasure.

Sometimes the slightest change
  can shift everything.
As I awaken to my emotions,
  may I be opened to be free.

Should I find myself stuck or overwhelmed,
  may I remember to feel them
in my body
  and breathe.

Uniting head and heart,
  may I come to trust their guidance,
  catch their glow, and
  ride their energy.

Emotions are the fuel of my creation.
May I harness them boldly
  to build the best of me.

Every day I have the option
   to inhabit a new self.
A river of constant motion
   flows one day and dream of me into the next.

In this sacred journey
   I do not have to know the
      destination, but only
   that what's being emptied daily
      is creating space for me
         to receive.

By going with the flow
   and trusting the current,
   May I come to love myself more deeply
      where I am,
         and in who I will be.

Love, love is the question
   to which I am the answer.

monlam 05

Today is the best day,
  as it is the only one I have.
With no regrets, may I lovingly
  cherish it, as I do myself.
This present moment is
  my creative canvas:
  to what does it invite me?
May I greet it with a fresh face
  and a beginner's mind.
Remembering that I'm OK and perfect,
  just as I am, that blank page
  reflects back my light, and
    beckons me to move.
Through the excitement of life
  and the value of my emotions,
I touch my creative core.
May everything respond differently
  as I fashion the space to grow.
Aware of my choices, and
  a Universe that conspires to bring me the best,
By means of this sacred work,
  may I meet myself in new and daring ways.

Hello—
You brighten my widening skies
  as we sit side-by-side.
How did I not notice
  something so beautiful?

Two faces of the same coin:
  I'm glad to have made your acquaintance
  as I sculpt a new life from within.

You are listening...
  I hear your voice like Garuda wings.
A certain sense of serenity arises as
  I come to see a multitude of things.
A thousand new eyes to view —
  You who know me best.

Be here with me. Take my hand.
  Whisper words that pause me, and arouse alignment.
Gently guide me to remember all I have forgotten,
  and the promise of what has yet to emerge.

"Life is what you make it,"
  I clearly heard you say.
No purpose to be "found"
  Outside the one which I create.

A portal has been opened,
  The invitation clearly accepted.
May I remember your instructions:
  "Breathe. Be present. Smile."

So simple, yet profound,
  I listen with curiosity and
  a new sense of wonder.

Each conversation with you is
  a loving step into new awareness,
  an emergence of receptivity, and
  a bolder assertion of trust
    that I can instill ardor into life.

Inner voice, font of wisdom reconciling the worlds,
  Awaken in me a fierce desire
    to love and know myself
      in ever more powerful ways.

monlam 08

To see the familiar with
  new eyes is both blessing
  and curse.
But curses are broken with awareness:
  today is a good day — may the blessing flow.

A fog has lifted,
  the veil has been rent.
Through the oracle of reflection
  I beheld, felt something
  I had missed, forgotten.

What are the features of my original face
  layered behind, beyond the one
    reflected back at me?
Curiously I gazed until the answer
  became clear and
    the revelation like a song.

Hello old one and ever fresh.
  Shattered—in a second
  that embrace took hold.
I stared into the eyes of my beloved,
  and there was delivered a key.

May this vision become fully rooted—
  Self-love is opening, the mystery beyond mastery—
  and through it may I be healed and renewed.

Just for today,
    may I live as if the outcome doesn't matter.

At this time,
    may I be free of expectation in myself and others.

In this moment,
    may I find satisfaction in free, creative flow.

Right now,
    may I simply breathe in and be.

To whatever arises,
    may I say "Yes!" and move forward in trust.

I shall come back to the present,
when I notice I'm in my head.
Sometimes the monsters
don't dwell under my bed.

May I come to find,
despite what I might believe,
Thoughts are simply that,
and pay the inner critic no heed.

Simple words:
  On a page,
  In my heart,
  Falling from my lips.

May they always be
  Direct, honest, and carefully chosen
  To move the spirit, still the mind,
    and create love in action.

monlam 12

What am I willing to lose, to risk
  so as to boldly emerge?

Who am I willing to be, to epitomize
  so as to powerfully serve?

Why am I willing to let go, to trust
  so as to freely create?

How am I willing to express, to explore
  so as to deeply live?

 I pray to embody the answer
  and soar on the wings of love.

monlam 15

Intuition, my returning friend,
  I seek wisdom from you again.
Never apart from me,
  you give eyes so that I may clearly see:
the visions that arise from deep inside,
  my trusted guide.
May I always listen for your voice,
  in the pause of silence.

Spark of initiation,
    Tongue of flame,
Voice of wisdom:
beyond name or label,
    Be with me.
As I make daring moves,
    take inspired action, and
    create new things;
Be my constant companion
    and caring guide.

Connecting to your energy, and
    offering the harvest of my best:
    I can move into unknowing with trust.
Aligned with you,
    I can bring forth something new
    and totally wondrous.

With an open heart,
    big smile, and
    deep breath,
I make a home for you, O Intuition,
    — here, you are always welcome.

monlam 15

Sometimes
I feel like there is no ground beneath my feet.
    Allow me to spread my wings and fly.

Sometimes
I know that there is no choice but to destroy.
    Allow me to see the new space and create.

Sometimes
I am stuck in fear and resistance.
    Allow me to lean in and open my heart.

Sometimes
I just need to let go and let be.
    Allow me to emerge in trust.

And sometimes
I remember my power and the ability
    of self-love to heal.
        And I breathe in deeply, smile radiantly,
            and placidly rest in this present moment.

In all these times, O Higher Self,
    be ever present.

As I slow down, I can
   step aside from my well-worn path.

When I'm still, I can
   draw from a more intimate source.

May I grant myself this space.

As I relinquish control, I can
   notice that I'm guided for better.

With no outcome to obtain, I can
   rest in a more noble purpose.

May I grant myself this peace.

In surrender, I am not lessened:
I am fully opened to receive.
   And then — only then —
All things will be given, for I've
   prepared the soil for soul to blossom,
     and watered it with my attention.

May I grant myself this trust.

monlam

All Good—

When shall I release,
That to which outside I cling?

My soul is aching for change.
May the way be cleared.

Moved: I am touched and pivot.
Melted: I am opened and allow.
Morphed: I am transformed and embody
    an even more powerful abandon—

In letting go of what no longer serves,
    of who I've thought myself to be,

Allow me to find refuge
    in what I so earnestly seek
    is only to be found in Me.

monlam 18

Today is a good day,
   to receive a gift of my own choosing.
The past is never dead. It's not even past,
   until I choose to relinquish, and bury it with grace.

Today is a good day to let go:
   of all the mistakes, all the hurts,
   all shoulds, and oughts, and could haves.

Everything, so that something new may sprout
   in the vacated space of regrets.

With heartfelt love,
   I now return any energy that I may have taken
   to its source with love and peace.

With mindful awareness,
   I call back any of my own power given away,
   that wholeness and balance may be restored to me.

In surrender and trust, may I remember my true name,
   and walk the way of beauty with no regrets.

monlam

Words drop.
Mind settles.
Body rests.

I give myself
permission
to let go
and let be.

Divine Love,
allow me to receive
this gift
in the same measure
in which you give.

Infinite.
Spacious.
Free.

SHAMAN DREAM

Part vision and part expressed feeling,
this mandala crystallizes the hero's journey
through the underworld of death and
resurrection which I experienced in my
professional burnout and spinal injury
between 2018 and 2019. I met myself in
many new ways from the ecstatic to the
utterly terrifying, from the urge to life
to the acquiescence of final extinction.

Teachers arrive in these liminal moments
under various guises. With heartfelt
devotion, I acknowledge my field-trip
buddy and love, Joel Hilborn; my mentor
and doppelgänger, Peleg Top; and my
herbal and shamanic teacher,
Renee Crozier Prince.

As I open my eyes
  and my heart,
I see and feel a new world dawning.

A spark of initiative,
  fueled by dedication,
and preceded by a leap into the dark.

Divine Love,
Creative Free Spirit,
Thank you for enticing me
  to meet myself afresh.
As we walk this journey together,
  allow me to risk everything for love.

monlam 21

Inner wisdom,
Refreshing well of fruitful darkness
   and wider dreams,
Teach me to smile at fear.

Abundant source of vast awareness
   and ardent energy,
Teach me to discern what to remove,
   manage, or create.

As it's only love that draws us through,
Teach me to rest freely in the moment.

monlam 22

Wild Imagination:
Dappled tongue of inspiration and abandon,
Speak through me.

In your rhythm and your rhyme:
Dance my willing hand and supple body.

Spilling over your haughty brew:
Drown my mind with your nectared drought.

Destroying the fortress of hope and fear:
Wrap me in your lush embrace.

Finding solace in your colorful land:
Dare me to never leave.

Great Love,
Deep Wisdom,
Higher Self:

If I were to act without concern about consequence,
What would I dream or dare to do?

Give me the strength and the courage
To arise to the asks of the day.

If I were step out of the comfortable and habitual,
Would I allow myself the space for real change?

Allow my vision become vast,
So that it exhausts my resistance.

If I were to voice my deepest desire
Could that song inspire me to make my quest?

Inspire me to enchant my life, and
Embody my soul's creative purpose.

Shedding the skin of all that holds me stuck,
I can don the raiment of transfiguration.
I need only choose.
And today I choose love.

monlam 24

Deep Self:

May I hear your voice
    on the edges of whispers.
May I see your reflection
    in the shadows of things.
May I taste your wonder
    on the tongue of attention.
May I touch your immensity
    in the body of presence.
May I smell your fragrance
    on the fabric of experience.

In this moment and
    a myriad of arisings,
May I know Samsara and Nirvana
    are the same:
The only difference is my perception.

monlam 25

Curious may I remain,
Like a golden thread
   linking trust and creativity.

Confident may I stand
To break the curse spell of knowing
   and reveal the joy of free spirit.

Receptive may I be,
Like hands lifted to the heavens
to catch the self-arisen child
   of spontaneity.

Deliver me
Into the heart of flame.

Deliver me
From anger and blindness.

Deliver me
From the burden of shame.

Deliver me
Into healing and kindness.

Deliver me
Embrace of self-love.

With the rising of
   the Great Eastern Sun:
I take my mountain seat.*

In the dawn of
   basic sanity and goodness:
I reclaim my power.

Through the radiant force
   of inherent wakefulness:
I pacify my inner chaos.

By my commitment to practice,
   may I tend to the verdant garden of self-love.

Through the cultivation of truth,
   may I live in freedom:
     knowing my worthiness in the very
      marrow of my bones,
     and expressing creativity in every
      movement and breath.

*The mountain summit, enveloped by sky, also serves as the throne or
 seat of mighty beings, as well as the place from where great shamans
 or ancestor kings descend, bringing their protection to the people.

Breaking through
   the lick of flames and acrid smoke,
   the inner oasis of the critic,
May a space be revealed,
   arms to cradle abundance.

Allowing the fuel of judgement,
   shame, guilt; all the afflictive emotions
   to be consumed in the
     cauldron of attention.

May my heart be opened to receive,
   and know the Universe conspires
     to bless me,
   when I hold the door to my being
     wide to welcome it like a dear friend.

May I come to understand
   creativity as utter receptivity.
Divine Love,
   make your home in me.

Death by a thousand cuts —
    here lies the corpse of sufficiency.

Control through a thousand chains
    is the dominion if the critic.

Through the simple act of asking,
    all can be remedied.

The joy of giving is multiplied
    by allowing others the same.

If the only prayer I ever mutter
    is "Thank you," it will suffice.

Being true to myself,
    may I be to open to receive.

Sometimes the greatest act of courage
   is to fully concede the immensity of me.

No matter how deeply I may be wounded
   or how intensely the critic rages:
Interpenetrating it all is my luminous source.

In this simple act of remembrance:
May my joy be full.
May my heart overflow.
May the mirror reflect my true beauty.
May the blessing of being me be totally relished
   for I am worthy to receive and be seen.

In this moment, everything is perfect:
   just as it is, ***just as I am.***

monlam 51

It's a new day—
    It's a new me.
I'll pay attention,
    and notice the signs.

A playlist of happiness,
    and tools in my box,
With an artist to guide me,
    I can't get lost.

I'll stay curious,
    find the syncs.
Keep opening to love,
    and all it brings.

May I find myself the temple,
    and act from this space.
Deep into my journey
    for the pilgrimage home.

monlam 32

Release.
  Accept.

As within,
  so without.

In all manner
  of things—

Celebrate.

I am being drawn
  in new ways through new lines
with every pen stroke,
  every art work.

In this cosmic game,
  may I remain ever more curious,
    have a hearty laugh,
  and hug myself just a little more tenderly...
Each day.

I am
Love. Whole. Enough.

My experience
Is the growth of joy.

My gift
Is the energy to receive.

My worth
Is the flow of desire.

I am
Life. Light. Creation.

Let me fail.
Let me fail at pleasing,
    so that I can serve.
Let me fail at expectations,
    for I know that I am enough.
Let me fail at perfection,
    embracing mistakes to learn.

May the spirals and crooked lines,
    funky colors and crossed-out words
be the composition that colors my world.

Between bliss and despair
    lies a single decision.
May I follow my clarion call.

From hurricanes to showers;
       from cacophony to a simpler tune—
Let the intensity be lessened.

With wider pauses and larger spaces,
       Let me be unstuck and with better options.

From director to player;
       from abuser to reminder—
Let the roles be reversed.

With restful nights and happier heart,
       Let me dwell in deeper contentment.

From overwhelm to direction;
       from derision to guidance—
May boundaries be held and expansion increase.

monlam 56

Resistance lets you know
　the revolution is here.
Against what do I wish to rebel?

The answer I will carefully choose,
　as if the very act will determine
　my fate — for surely it will.

How I do anything is how
　I show up to everything.
Today, what will it be?

May I have the resolve and
　the strength to choose me,
　to embrace the deeper love.

When the prison door is open,
　then, then is the time to leave.
That door is now open.

Open.
Let me take the next step,
　fueled by the words
　I no longer need, and will not receive.

Let me craft a new language
evoking the world I will speak into being
　of kaleidoscopic eyes, bold strokes,
　　and an even more ardent desire.

System Upgrade

THE ENNEAGRAM'S SOUL ASSURANCES

The Enneagram is a fascination of mine.
Shrouded in mystery and lore, no one knows
if it is the encapsulation of an ancient doctrine
of the psyche or a more modern invention.
Regardless, I have found it to be a powerful
system of psychological and spiritual growth.
In fact, when presented with my personality
type, revelation ensued. I finally understood
my basic driving fear and was presented
with the soul assurance, a mantra of sorts,
that provides a pathway to integration and
a means to reconnect with my sacred spark.
The assurances presented here are in the
language fittingly describing an upgrade
to the human operating system.

Does one in particular resonate with you?

monlam 57

Time to upgrade the system,
  write some new code.

The current system isn't inadequate:
  a few lines got degraded along the way.

Let me reboot
  with a fresh, new interface.

Hello, Good,
  will give you the power
    to do more of the things you love,
  and do *you* like never before.

monlam 58

In an environment of duality,
    ask for mutuality.
It's not rejection if it's not the right yes.

Leave the door open,
    erase the past cache of memory.
The universe makes no mistakes.

Hello, Wanted,
    allows you to express your treasure,
and your essential desire, wholeness.

I embrace my hardware:
    Touch my keys.
Let the power flow,
    while the world explodes before me
    as a gospel of love and abundant attraction.

monlam 59

/Open up to the delicious loop:
   Take in the night.
Bring in the day.

Engineered to go all out:
   what you are
   is how you'll come to be.

Hello, Loved 4BNU,
   unfolds your essence as
the delight of the manifold multiverse.

Shooting love though my circuits,
   let me shed a filament of light
     into the darkness
   and unfurl the colors of my soul.

May I be love(d) for who I am —
   original innocence and authenticity —
The calling card to reap the infinite joys of life.

monlam

Disconnect from the advertising trope:
There is no-thing more
   or an add-on you require.

Already plugged in and
   running well with electric fire,
Rip off the plastic and be received.

Hello, BScene,
   allows you to radiate your own grandeur
Upon your alluring big life screen.

Let me envy my own connection:
   without this satisfaction
The whole system crashes.

May I recognize the beauty
   I so eagerly see(k)
Is the appreciation of my own reflection.

With all the questions to be deciphered,
    the right answers to be discovered,
Withdraw for clarity...

Many maps illustrated the terrain,
    but be simple to arrive
At the heart of the matter.

Hello, Capable,
    decouples you from compulsive
    problem solving and the need to know,
And connects you to resting in mystery and
co-creation.

May I let go of the drive
    to find answers and solutions
And notice the assistance that surrounds me.

Let me trust my needs will never be a problem.
    /Ask, and I shall receive.

Running from fear,
        mired in doubt,
You need a sign or validation.

Structures of support to hide the anxiety,
        distraction from what is true in you.
Courage is your virtue.

Hello, Safety,
        exhausts the virus of external threats,
And connects you to the grid of inner fortifying trust.

May I avail my own resilience,
        and discern that everything
is working out for me.

Let me be grounded in
        abundance and assurance.
I am my own refuge, yet I am not alone.

monlam

Too many options to be explored,
   far-reaching plans to be made:
Anything to stave the inner ache.

Closure limits freedom,
   you will follow imagination
In flights of gluttonous fancy.

Hello, Satisfaction,
   will align you to the fructuous dynamism
   of the Universe,
And fulfill your every need.

May I harness my innate curiosity,
   and rest in the unplumbed silence,
Acceding to the intimacy of true self-care.

Let me occupy my pain and not run,
   I will not end when the pleasure does.
I will always be taken care of.

monlam

You walk before you crawl,
     and with anger push against everything.
The lust is for control.

Trust is earned,
     Many fucking messes are made.
Prices are paid — nothing is free.

Hello, Protection,
     allows you to live vulnerably from the heart,
And reveal your lofty dream and authentic core.

May I find my innocence is my strength,
     and love the stunted inner child
Who longs to come out and play.

Let me reclaim what was once lost,
     and allow myself to be held and loved,
For I will not be betrayed.

monlam 45

Every other garden tended,
    while yours lies fallow.
Witness without participation.

Diplomat and peacemaker,
    all come to rest in your infinite chill.
But anger is buried deep.

Hello, Significance,
    awakens you to the necessity of self-love
And plants you firmly in your unique position.

May I take my own needs as worthy,
    and no longer sacrifice myself
As martyr and mediator.

Let me right the trade-off of self-forgetting,
    and envelope myself in the depth of love.
I am the crux, center, and circumference.
I matter, and I am love(d).

Bardo Scenes

ENTER THE LIMINAL —
THE SPACES IN BETWEEN

I use a smattering of Tibetan terms in my
writing, as I have been a student and practitioner
of Tibetan Buddhism (Vajrayana) for nearly
30 years. Foreign words stimulate the mind, and
add nuance that is not possible in the English
language. Bardo, translates to "space between"
life phases, of which there are six in the Buddhist
cosmology: birth and life, the dream state,
meditative absorption, the moment of death,
luminosity of the true nature, and becoming
(or transmigration). In the process of spiritual
awakening, we will find ourselves in many
of these liminal spaces.

What are you between?

Aligned and
  guided,
A simple
  spark
awakens the
  blaze,
torches fear,
  and renders
you
One more
  step closer
to home.

9 facets,
  1 gem

That is you.

May you be
  set in the
place that
  befits you the
most.

Love.

monlam 47

Welcome, Artist.
"Wear
    your hat."

Let me claim my
  right to move
through the world
in this way
  crystalize the flow
    of the energy of Love.

May I be enriched
  and choose
my word —
title my life and work.

Let each experience,
  uncover,
unpeel,
a little bit more,
  excavate the more
obvious, and excite the
  remembrance of who I am.

May I stay curious,
  pick my colors, begin
to follow creative free spirit, and
  play, frolicking with my
    Inner Artist.   69

monlam 18

Often, the
greatest prayer is the
simple moment, resting
in quiet
presence.

Breathing in this
moment,
  pliant whisk of a
loaded
 brush or
fluid pen.

Let
          me   flow:
artist of
meaning-filled life —
on roads,
in crevasses   between
thought   and
            expression.

monlam 49

in the silence of love
the mind relaxes into
its natural state
like the leaf to
the wind
and the heart
bubbles forth
a gurgling spring.

neither too loose
nor too tight
a soft symphony
ensues like
lovers embrace.

release and
transformation occur
in the point
where I am willing
to both die and open
just a bit more.

may I awaken this
ecstatic dance
in each moment
each breath
each thought
each feeling
free as it is reborn.

Timeframes of
significance.

Memories of
the present.

May each
give blush to
my recollection of
the future.

Creative Free Spirit,
...let's play!

Inspiration
Freely flow.

Your present breath
Ignites flame.
Creative action.
Cries my name.

Returning the gaze
I playfully allow myself to be.
More than enamored.
Fusion sparks.

Tending the other as a garden
Earthy hands
And loamy soil to
The artist soul.

May we birth each
Other in joy.

Crafting a new
  raiment,
One that fits
  —more beautifully designed
for lightness of heart,
  neon spirit,
curious creativity,
  living magic,
coils of connection,
  pleromas of purpose.

So let it be.
  Me.

wheel of fortune
  given a spin
regardless where it lands
  where does my satisfaction begin?

no need of a distant future
  or a horizon to pass
boldly drinking back the courage
  my destiny will commence.

shrink before fear,
  or emerge immense.

evening.
summer storm.
back porch.
cool breeze.

kind words.
inspiration flash.
emotional surge.
just resting.

pastel stroke.
present moment.
loving touch.
special moment.

self love.

what a beautiful
  thing that just happened.

from deep inside
  I touched my voice
a song of bone
  and electric pulses
and scenic possibilities
  within a finger-length
and even closer.

honey-tongued
  received like cold tears
from swollen summer sky
  let me rest my
beautiful head and
  star-glinted eyes
before a single thought
  could ever awaken
another dream.

what a beautiful
  life that is just lived.

be the kind of
  person who gets excited
over the stars at night.

one who knows
  his trail is trodden like
foamy waves across oceans.

be the kind of
  person who finds life
in the practice of love.

one who asks
  tell me more
rather than running away.

be the kind of
  person who rests content
for all is well, all is well.

 monlam

There is a felicity
  to devotion that
quenches the thirst
  for love.

That is why
  I wake early
for a thousand mornings
  to dream a house
of light.

There, there where
  I can serve
over many miles
  and moons
just a singular moment.

Let me take
  no virgin voyage
but the pilgrimage
  home to cherish all
others by first
  embracing myself.

Relax
into who
you
really are
right
now.

Past
your breath,
the cover
of your skin
is already
too far.

Breathe
into that
unfathomable,
edgeless
space:
Ready

ready to
receive.
You are
the guest
of opulent
abundance.

The table
has always
been set.
Sup with
abandon
from the
quiet riches

you have
now uncovered
from the
cache of
your heart.

Growth isn't
always measured
by a forward motion
or a critique of quantity.

More often it is
better assessed
in thoughtful words,
the circumference of edges,
and the willingness
to occur

like the curious child
playing for the first time,
everytime,
without judgement,
let me recollect
the wonder
of how the acorn
becomes the oak.

Treading the vital arc,
Accept the invitations
That alight upon the way.

Everybody gets shine;
Each in their own time.
Boldly decorate your stay.

through this time and practice,
may we come into the fullness of self-love
and alight our blaze.

may we continue
to be empowered, enriched,
and grateful.

may we enjoy the abundance
of what is before us, but even more
of what we already house and hold.

may we bear courageous witness
to power shared, and may
all obstacles to our life and success,
become fuel for our journey.

may all be auspicious,
may all be well.

monlam 62

a flickering fiat
   is abundance.

drawn like
   pulsing flame
to punctuating wings,
a thousand photons
   entangled with
a radiant sun.

elusively lured
   away,
forgetful of that
   single point
from which it is
   thrown and escapes:
an eventful horizon.

perchance may
   I discover
no difference
   exists, and
I am the
   spectrum
which displays
   the fullness of
its source.

barefoot roaming
cool forest floors

ample funds
sphere of influence

path to my study
traipsing through the house

love: appreciative and lusty
distinctive visage

midnight skinny dip
hidden sweet kisses

trusted secrets
true friends

abundance appears
with many faces and arms

relish the cartography
of your soul

monlam 64

Find before you seek.
Receive before you give.
Die before you live.

Grab the rung.
Question the usual.
Believe in yourself.

Between excitation and rest,
Abundance flows.
Greet the day afresh.

Words have worth
like a flock of geese
  driven by instinct home.

Staccato cries break
across clear sky which
frames the spectacle
  of their course.

Chosen wisely
  a pearled offering feast
  or a seismic clarion call.
but rashly uttered
  the shattering of the vital chords
  or the penitentiary bangles of beliefs.

String your syllables —
momentous malas of meaning —
as galactic arms

And seed the interior star
of your own gravity and glow.

monlam 66

pay attention.

look for the opportunities:
  the pauses

and

  the breaks.

each bardo
  asks you just
one question.

between this   and   that
whom shall I be?

montra 67

*I believe in
MAGIC.
And because
I believe in
MAGIC,
There is always
MAGIC
In my life.

I experience
ABUNDANCE.
And because
I experience
ABUNDANCE,
There is always
ABUNDANCE
In my life.

I LOVE
myself.
And because
I LOVE
myself,
There is always
LOVE
In my life.

The
MAGIC
Of
ABUNDANCE
Is
LOVE.

* I believe in giving credit where credit is due; however, I cannot verify
the source of this beautiful and presonally meaningful magic mantra
upon which the others are based. I think if may be a quote of Armen Ra,
the renowned thereminist and performer.

monlam 68

The effect is
  the cause:
there is no
  other *way*.

A thought
  otherwise is a simple
trick of the mind
  staking its claim.

A simple crack
  in the machinations:
a window allows
  the glimmer escape.

Walk a mile in the
  souls of your feet
and the journey is nearly finished
  before you ever take a step.
The morning dawn rises
  from a singular sacrifice:
the blue marble surrenders
  to the gravity as
her trajectory traverses
  her source.

ordinary moments
  —no such things.
inbox notification.
  morning drive memories.
another Zoom call.

curiosity uncovers value
  in spaces others
rarely encounter or
  at worst ignore.

the first page
  sets the tone
for all the novel turns
  to the chapters
of your difference.

take your heart
 from your sleeve
and wear in in your hands.
  quick to give
joyful to receive.

purpose is a scripture
  to be read
from eyes,

wise to the wonder
  of their why.

91

More than
accolades of
adoring fans.

More than
the roar of money
printing machines.

More than
tick marks on
a list of goals.

More than
the magic to
manifest your will.

Is a simple
measure of
success.

Having done
your best,

are you
satisfied?

Clean up
In aisle Psyche.

Negative
Self-talk spill.

Liberate
This eruption.

Rewrite
Your story.

Create
Amazing habits.

Retrieve
Your power.

Wounds
Are where the
Light comes through.

Tell the
World

Why
You are enough.

There is no language
that describes who
you really are.

What I'm noticing
are points of convergence
and intimation of value.

Gods rarely ever send
a postcard,
an owner's manual.

We may never look for
this, but we're
seen every minute.

The absurdity of this
singular thought
can be revealed in silence.

No requirements involved.
Purpose seeks you:
and it will consume.

In this moment of recognition
everything finds you.

Canvas
Paint
Masterpiece

Yacht
Hammer tap
Expert fees

Ideas
Brewing
Dreams

Abundance
Bursting
Seams

May I dare
Become who
I am.

Simple words
  enliven the soul
and set the course.

What's your direction?

Clarity blooms
in fertile hearts
who long
to be free,
know they
are love(d),
and refuse
to hide their light.

In the hours
of days,
keep the
channel open.

Inhabit the
ecology of
your experience.

Do more
than keep
your word:
make it
incarnate.

The listening
is epiphany,
and silence
to be seen.

I am my project.
Nothing to fix.
Nothing to do
  except abide in me.

From doing to being:
fixing what isn't broken,
healing what's already whole
  is the paradox of the entire exercise.

Drawing down the bones
  and capturing the connections
is the ritual of the awakened.

Nothing has changed,
  yet everything is different.

One cannot lead
  who has not first
    surrendered.

Surrendered to the
  encompassing singular desire
    that holds the critical voice
  at bay.

For it is only the
  darkness before the dawn
    which announces the
  glory of the unfolding day.

monlam 78

Dark winter matter
fills the gaps between
pregnant, pulsing neural nodes
and galactic arms.

Across the expanse
of the cosmos,
I cradle in my heart the
hidden light of distant stars.

Knowing this present magic
I weld my words
and fashion for all who would hold it,
a world in which all is fully lived.

The precision
of attention
is a characature
of simple noticing.

An interview
teasing out details
clearly written
upon a face.

Proximity cannot
mimic the intimacy
of connection.

Tailor your
foundations bespoke
to thoughtfully engineer
a family of us.

Awareness
of the prison
is the only way
to find the key.

afternoon serkyem to the protectors

Whatever the
opportunity,
challenge,
is only born
in the strength
of our weakness

smoke whisps of juniper incense

Crack the secret
of learning to be led
if you truly
want to lead.

Caught in a new zone,
Evoke your archetype
and inhabit home.

Tap the power
of the roles within:
Lover, sage, magician.

Revelation once received,
keys to the kingdom,
Simple to believe.

We're gifted with the chance
to write our own book of life,
the scripture of our
experience and existence.

Letter by letter,
images and memories,
flooding and filling
each expressive page.

Notes on the sidebars,
mistakes and spills,
triumphs and edits,
chapters like blockbusters.

Craft your pages well,
and hide nothing
so that your beauty
shines through.

Don't worry about the title.
It will find you.

Essen(ce)tial

A GRIMºIRE of BLªZING GLºRY

The teachings of theEnneagram appear
again ... now as a grimoire of essential
secrets, a book of words of worth to reveal
one's innate wisdom, power, and love.
At is core, the Enneagram is spiritual path
to wholeness, integration, and presence.
May these words evoke the memory of
your essence and awaken your aspiration
to arise from the slumber of culture and
the fixation of personality.

monlam

Let drop the shackles
  of burdensome ideals.

And allow yourself to
  be a disciple of joy.

Discern your perfection
  through acceptance and allowance.

All is whole and serene
  when judgement is dropped.

Playfully sparked and blooming in rest,
  your manifold goodness manifests.

You have treasure
to reveal—look inside.

Honor your own needs
and feel the freedom you find.

There is no commodity to love,
so give in to the flow.

You are wanted,
and every atom dances about you.

No conditions or demands accompany
this basic paradox:

the vast universe containing all
is incomplete without you.

Enjoy being yourself
for everyone else is taken.

No wheel of masks
or roles to play.

You are authentic in your being,
and not your doing *(which you do so well).*

Unfurl the colors of your soul
where your value dwells.

How you arrive is important:
Show up a vessel of love.

monlam 86

Stay present and
express the your heart truth.

No drama, nothing to judge,
and no rescue required.

Don't take the bait — feelings aren't facts,
just ornaments of experience.

In every meaning-filled moment,
you are seen for who you are.

Underneath we share the same significance,
distinct images of the creative divine.

monlam

Invite the mind into this, your body,
and come back home.

Power and control betray
the primacy of trust.

Clarity coruscates in the vastness
from which all arises.

Only in the body of life
can sanctuary be found.

Grounded in the flow of this dance,
your needs are not a conundrum.

Pause—the cosmos
conspires for your good.

Abide in this mystery
and sojourn in its attention.

Discard the cacophony of voices
who never substantiate support.

For answers you seek—depart
the anxious, pull back your skin.

Know this in your bones,
infallible as the certain Ground.

Cradle your faith through knowing
You are safe.

monlam 89

The richness of the present moment
is only tasted in silence.

In this playground,
not every ride is to be ridden.

Stop and metabolize your pain—
don't medicate with plans of the future.

Dance in joy, as this
ecstacy is your birthright.

Unwrap the gift of life
with unceasing, shared gratitude.

With everything taken care of,
your touch makes the ordinary divine.

You have my word on this:
I empower and respond.

Outer control is just a mimicry
of generosity and self-mastery.

Vulnerability is the truest power:
no walls to impede the transformation of rage.

Surrendering to the heart of trust,
essential strength emerges.

Emboldened by a larger cause,
I become a vessel of purpose.

The natural order of things is innocent,
and here, I will not be betrayed.

The Universe makes no mistakes,
  so stop postponing your life.

Take a fresh start, possessed
  by the gravity of your own worth.

No self-erasing mask of rage
  to hide the love well bubbling forth.

By your nature enlivened, you hold
  in tender hands the paradox of connection.

Relish this electric body, and give eyes
  to the reflection mirror'd back and seen.

You matter because you are you,
  And your are love(d).

Bloom!

Every Ending Is A New Beginning

RETURNING from the PILGRIMAGE

Having made the epic quest, the pilgrimage
to the site of the sacred, my hero's journey,
the road seemingly comes to an end, initiation
complete. However, my journey is actually
just beginning. Decorated in the glow
of purification, satisfaction, and
accomplishment, I return home,
heart laurel-ladened and full.

Where do I go from here?
Walk with Divine Love and Creative Free Spirit
— see where you go!

the empty page
 an invitation
its mirror-like intensity,
 dappled, mute surface
lures me, teases me
 to engage.

"What will you make of me?"
 it screams in a whisper.
I think the better-asked question:
 "What will you make of me?"

monlam 93

I know which one
  I like better.

The slap of word
  across arctic white sheet.
Voices of elated cadence
  falling staccato drops
into heart and ear.
Blocked, vivid chalk:
  emotions drawn onto space.

I know which one
  I like better.

Finish line
  within clear sight.
Lingering doubts
  shrinking fearful back;
A final teasing joust
  delivers the upper hand.

I know which one
  I like the better.

Every one which
  shepherds me home,
that leads me
  twisty-lined unswerving.
Back to my own arms —
  an ardent lover.

monlam 94

Visceral sigh,
   pause, relief,
an initiation complete.

Akin to ancient fires,
   I've crafted a new myth
to rewild my soul.

What's been shed
   like serpent skin
allows a new heart beat.

Draw near,
   I've new magic
to bring dawn to night.

A hundred days from now,
  whom shall I be?

Let me carry that *kōan*,
  like my dog's favorite bone:

Sucking out the marrow,
  grinding it completely down.

Welcome the surprise,
  you will be fed succulent words.

An answer to a question
  that cannot be voiced.

But appears just the same —
  just to be noticed,

before disappearing, slipping
  away, to a great depth inside of me.

A hundred days from now,
  whom shall I be?

I Create With My Words

BLESSINGS FOR THE JOURNEY

Affirming our deepest natures,
acknowledging our heart-felt gratitude,
and aspiring for the highest expressions
of love and creativity, these words are
offered as blessings along the way.

blessing 01

In times of trouble, or times of joy,
Whatever the occasion:

Come, walk with me.
Neither of us may know the way,
        but our hearts will lead us home.

Here, sit with me.
Let us toast our dreams and aspirations,
        as the world seems a little heavy.

Now, now is the time.
In this moment, let us simply enjoy our company,
        for tomorrow never comes.

And if it did, could it ever compete,
        with us who've taken the time to be,
        to rest, to listen and smile.
    Something new will never replace
        the simple satisfaction of the moment
        we've spent and pleasantly savored.

Time quickly comes to pass
        so let us appreciate our sacred scene.
    May we always have sweet arms to hold
        and lips to speak,

"Thank you for being you, and the pleasure
        of being me."

blessing 02

Divine Love:

The way has its dangers and its delights:
  and you give me all that I need, and I am open
  to receive.

The way of the Mystic is the path of unknowing:
  may I develop trust and curiosity.

The way of the Warrior is the path of courage:
  may I tame fear and make it my ally.

The way of the Sage is the path of inner knowing:
  may I cultivate intuition and insight.

The way of the Magician is the path of power:
  may I deftly wield creativity and harness emotion.

The way of the Lover is the path of passion:
  may I embrace life in all its manifestations,
  and appreciate myself in fullness.

blessing 05

THE SIX NAILS OF TILOPA*

Don't recall. The past has passed.

Don't imagine. Let go of what may arise.

Don't think. Let go of what is happening right now.

Don't examine. There is nothing to figure out.

Don't control. Let whatever happen.

Rest. Relax, let the mind rest in its natural state.

*The Six Nails of Tilopa *is a traditional Vajrayana Buddhist pointing out instruction on the nature of mind by the mahasiddha Tilopa. This blessing is based upon the translation by Ken McLeod.*

blessing

*

May you have every happiness.

*

May you be free of every suffering.

*

May you know love, joy, and peace.

*

May creativity and abundance be your beauty way.

*

May you walk, poised and courageous,
with self-love and compassion,

knowing the treasure of your life,
and the magic of seasons and days.

*

When you find yourself asleep,
may you quickly notice, apply the antidotes
(of presence and acceptance),
and gently move on.

*

Until next we meet again,
may all auspiciousness be yours!

*

129

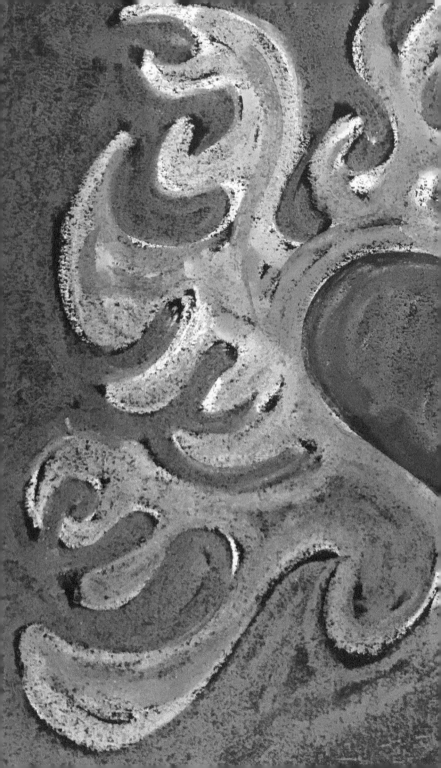

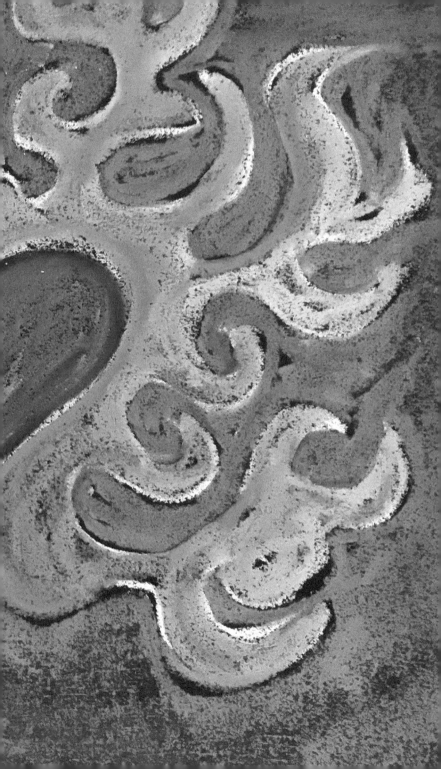

About the Author

Ericson AF Proper is a brand developer and graphic designer who has worked with multiple clients over the past 25 years to distill their essence, develop a visual language to communicate their unique attributes, and create lasting impact. From individuals to large corporations, he has served curiosity, dry humor, saturated color, and measurable results since 2005 through his award-winning and cheekily titled studio, Properganda. He also relishes publication design, having been creative director over 10 highly regarded regional lifestyle magazines from 2000 through 2005.

Inspired by the 100 Days of Creative High Growth process, he now brings the unique insights and skills of his graphic career to transformational coaching and spiritual direction: a familiar return to the call of his soul first explored as a Roman Catholic seminarian in the late 80's.

At the intersection of creativity, spirituality, and magic, he works with individuals in transition and liminal spaces to discover their innate wisdom. Within a safe, alchemical container of trust, curiosity, deep inquiry, and love, he guides each individual to reconnect with their inner magic to achieve powerful results.

Outside of his day work, Ericson an accomplished photographer, meditation and Qigong teacher, and practices in several spiritual lineages. His continuing study and practice of herbalism and traditional healing, the Enneagram, and Jyotish is conducted from his home, in Lakeland, Florida, which he shares his husband, Joel, and two loving pets.

For more information on Ericson's coaching practice, classes, and teaching visit **ericsonproper.com**.

CPSIA information can be obtained
at www.ICGtesting.com
Printed in the USA
BVHW090008181120
593549BV00004B/178

9 781087 911038